MW00811449

Revelations
to the
Shepherd of Hermas

"You have a great and important ministry,"
the angel said. "...your task is to tell people
the commandments of God."

Revelations

to the
Shepherd of Hermas

*A Book
of Spiritual Visions*

Compiled by Robert Van de Weyer

Triumph™ Books
Liguori, Missouri

1-800- 328 - 4648

Augburg (Fax) 1-800- 722-7766

Published by Triumph™ Books
Liguori, Missouri
An Imprint of Liguori Publications

All rights reserved. No part of this publication may be reproduced, stored in a retrieval system, or transmitted in any form or by any means—electronic, mechanical, photocopy, recording, or any other— except for brief quotations in printed reviews without the prior permission of the publisher.

Library of Congress Cataloging-in-Publication Data

Hermas, 2nd cent.
  [Shepherd. English. Selections]
   Revelations to the Shepherd of Hermas : a book of spiritual visions / compiled by Robert Van de Weyer. — 1st U.S. ed.
      p.   cm.
   Originally published: The Shepherd of Hermas : an apocalypse. Evesham, Worcestershire [England] : Arthur James, 1995.
      ISBN 0-7648-0054-X
      1. Private revelations. 2. Christian life.   I. Van de Weyer, Robert.   II. Title.
BS2900.H4A3   1997
229'.93—dc21   96-39141

Originally published in English by Arthur James Ltd., Publishers, under the title *The Shepherd of Hermas: An Apocalypse.*

Text © 1995 Robert Van de Weyer
© 1995 Arthur James Ltd.

Printed in the United States of America
First U.S. Edition 1997
97 98 99 00 01   5 4 3 2 1

Introduction

The theme of *The Shepherd of Hermas* is of perennial interest to all Christians: how to live up to the standards which Christ set, and how to recover after failure and sin mar the soul. Many Christians in the decades after Christ's death believed that it was possible after baptism to lead a perfect and sinless life; and some even held that a sin committed by a baptized Christian could not be forgiven. Hermas wanted to uphold the spiritual and moral ideals of the Gospel, but recognized that Christians remain prey to sinful impulses; and throughout his book he grapples in different ways with this paradox.

The book is in the form of an apocalypse, similar to the final book of the New Testament, consisting of a series of revelations made to Hermas. Each revelation is followed by an explanation, which draws out its practical and ethical purpose. The early chapters are a series of visions in which Hermas first meets a woman called Rhoda, whose slave Hermas may have been; then he meets an old woman, and finally a beautiful young woman. It becomes clear that these three women represent the Church; and Hermas is given a message by them, which he must convey to the leaders of the Church, rebuking them for their greed and hypocrisy. The central character of the book now appears, a handsome young man dressed as a shepherd, who gives Hermas twelve commandments. Finally, Hermas is caught up in a series of parables or allegories, in which every figure and object has a symbolic meaning. Even today these parables are both fascinating and deeply disturbing.

The Shepherd of Hermas appeared in one of the early canons of the Scriptures, but was eventually dropped because its author was assumed to have no apostolic connections.

This judgment was almost undoubtedly correct: the book was probably written over a period of years from about A.D. 125 onward, so the author is unlikely to have met any of the apostles. Nonetheless it continued to circulate widely, and was revered by many as a work of profound truth.

Today it is virtually unread. The style is at times convoluted and awkward, and, besides, the apocalyptic form is quite alien to the modern mind. This present version of *The Shepherd of Hermas* is not a direct translation, but is an attempt to make the text and its meaning more accessible—and thus bring out the profound wisdom and vivid imagery which it contains.

ROBERT VAN DE WEYER

I grew up as a slave, and when I was a young man my owner sold me to a woman called Rhoda in Rome. As the months and years passed, I began to love Rhoda. Once I saw her bathing in the river Tiber, I gave her my hand to help her out of the water. When I saw her beautiful body rising out of the water, I said to myself, "I would be happy if I had a wife of such beauty and character." This was my only thought; no feelings of lust passed through my mind. Some time later, when I was traveling to Cumae, I suddenly felt very sleepy, and lay down at the side of the road. I looked up at the sky and the trees, and was overwhelmed with the splendor and the beauty of God's creation. Then my eyes closed. While I was asleep a spirit seized me, and took me away to a remote district where the ground was so rocky and the hills so steep that it was impossible to walk. The spirit put me down on one side of the river. I swam across the river, and on the other side I found soft, level ground. I knelt down, and began to confess my sins to the Lord. While I was praying the heavens opened, and I saw Rhoda, the woman whom I desired as my wife.

2

I looked up to heaven, and again I was overwhelmed by Rhoda's beauty. "What are you doing here, dear lady?" I asked. "I was taken up to heaven to charge you with your sins before the Lord," she answered. "Are you accusing me?" I asked. "No," she said, "but listen carefully to the words I am going to say to you. God, who dwells in heaven and who created the universe out of nothing, is angry with you because you sinned against me. You pretended to look upon me as a goddess, treating me with the utmost respect. But in truth you desired me for yourself. You imagine that outward actions are all that matter; but God can see the thoughts and desires of the heart. You wanted me not only for my beauty, but for my wealth and my status. You were no better than those evil men who rape any woman they fancy and steal any goods they want. Now your life is worthless, because my accusation will ensure your condemnation. But there is hope. You must repent of your sins, and beg God to be healed."

After Rhoda had laid such terrible charges against me the heavens shut, and I found myself shaking with fear and grief. I said to myself: "If this sin is recorded against me, how shall I be saved? And if this sin is counted as so great, my numerous other sins must make me the vilest person that ever lived. What words can I use to win the Lord's forgiveness?" While these thoughts were filling my heart, a huge white chair made of lamb's wool appeared before me. Then an old woman, dressed in a shining robe and carrying a great book, sat on the chair. "Greetings, Hermas," the old woman said. "Why are you so gloomy? Normally you are cheerful, laughing freely, yet now you look utterly miserable." "It is because I have sinned against a most beautiful lady," I replied. She smiled at me, with kindness in her eyes, saying: "Certainly you have sinned, but you are not condemned. God allowed you to sin, because he wanted to show you the nature of sin. It was his design that you should be filled with fear and grief. Normally with your happy temperament and innocent joy you are totally oblivious to sinfulness. But now your eyes are starting to open."

4

I felt reassured by the old woman's words, yet also deeply puzzled. "Why should I be made to understand the nature of sin?" I asked. "The main cause of sin," she replied, "is not malice or ill will, but blindness. It is very rare for people deliberately to do harm to others; most people at most times imagine that they are doing good. But they are blind to their own distorted emotions, which infect their words and their actions. Those emotions cause them to say things which hurt and destroy others, and cause them to do things which deprive others of food and shelter, dignity and self-respect. When someone later accuses them of sin, they indignantly deny it. They cannot see the connection between their inner emotions and their outer actions. And they cannot see the connection between their own actions and the suffering of others. So the first step to repentance is for a person to see clearly the root of sin within the heart. Pray to God that he will open your eyes to discern this root in your heart."

The old woman paused, and she looked down to the ground with sadness in her eyes. I asked her why she was sad. "I must now say something that will hurt you deeply," she replied, "and I am looking into my heart to see that my motives are pure." "I trust you to speak with a pure heart," I said. "Then I shall speak," she answered. She lifted her head and fixed her eyes on mine. "All parents want to do the best for their children," she said, "and all parents hate the thought of harming their children. Yet because you have been blind to the nature of sin, you have corrupted your children. You have been self-indulgent toward them, not correcting them when they do wrong. For this reason the Lord is angry with you. But he will put right your errors, healing your children of their corruption. You, for your part, must change your ways. You imagine it is virtuous and kind to tolerate your children's bad behavior, because you do not have to hurt them by exerting discipline. It is not tolerance, but fear and sloth which lie behind your indulgence: you are frightened of your children's hostile reaction if you were to punish them, and you are too lazy to impose punishment. Thus you must pray to God that you can overcome your fear, and find strength and energy. Just as the blacksmith, hammering the hot iron, fashions it into the shape he desires, so righteous words and just punishment will fashion your children in the way God desires. Then the names of your children will be written in the great book of saints and kept in heaven."

6

When the old woman had finished speaking, I did not feel hurt, but rather I felt comforted and reassured. I knew that under God's guidance I would learn to repent. The old woman asked if I would like to hear her read aloud. I replied that I would. So she opened a great book and began reading from it. Much of what she read was very frightening to me, because it concerned the punishment which the wicked suffer; I have blotted these words from my memory. But then the words of the book became warm and gentle, and these I can remember. "Let us love the Lord God, who in his power and wisdom created the earth, as the supreme artist filled the world with objects and creatures of sublime beauty. Let us love the Lord God, who by his mighty Word created heaven, as the perfect repose for righteous souls. Let us love the Lord God, who in his love for all humankind created his holy Church, as the vehicle by which men and women can travel from earth to heaven. Let us love the Lord God, who in his mercy has given us his Son, Jesus Christ, who teaches us how to behave and invites us into the holy Church, so we can help one another obey his commands."

The old woman continued to read from the book. "Let us love one another, searching out the spark of divine love in every heart. Let us love one another, fanning that spark into a warm flame. Let us love one another, confessing openly and freely when we have done wrong. Let us love one another, forgiving without reserve the sins which others confess. Let us love one another, sharing with others the spiritual and material gifts which God has bestowed on us. Let us love one another, receiving with humility and gratitude the spiritual and material gifts which others offer. Let us love one another, praying that the words we speak may be guided by God's Spirit. Let us love one another, listening for the words of God's Spirit in the mouths of others." When the old woman had finished reading, she rose from the chair, touched me gently, and asked: "Did my reading please you?" "Lady," I replied, "the first part about the punishment which the wicked suffer was very hard for me to hear; but the second part about love pleased me greatly." "My dear Hermas," she said, "if you love God and love other people as instructed in the second part, you can ignore the first." Then she went away, and I awoke.

8

About a year after my first vision, when I was again walking along the road to Cumae, I lay down to rest at the same place as before. And as I fell asleep the spirit seized me, and took me to the place I had been the previous year. The old woman appeared, walking toward me and reading from a book. She said to me: "I will read the contents of this book, which you must repeat to the members of the holy Church." "Lady," I replied, "I cannot remember so much; hand me the book." She handed it to me, and I began to copy it letter by letter. As I am illiterate, I did not know the meaning of what I copied. It took me many weeks to complete the task, and throughout this time the old woman stood beside me. When I had finished the last letter, she took the book from me. Then she said: "The copy which you have made must be seen by no one except you." "But since I cannot read," I protested, "I shall never know what it means." "You do not need to know its meaning with your head," she said, "but only with your heart. By writing out every letter, the meaning of the book has gone into your heart. For the next fifteen days you must eat no food. You must devote yourself entirely to prayer, looking into your heart to discover what this book means." I felt perplexed, because I did not know how it was possible to read a book with the heart and not with the head. Then I realized that I understood the Bible with my heart, but in my head I was still baffled by much of it.

For fifteen days I ate nothing, and I drank only water. At first my stomach was desperate for food, and great pangs of hunger shot through my body. After a few days the pangs went, but my mind became desperate for food, thinking of nothing else but bread and meat. Finally, the hunger in my body and my mind disappeared, and my heart felt wonderfully pure. The meaning of the book was clearly visible within my heart, and it was very simple. If people repent this day of all past sins, they will be completely forgiven by God. But the offer will not be made a second time. From this day forward their lives must be blameless. In particular the leaders of the Church must repent of their sins of pride and greed, and give themselves entirely to the care of their flock. There must never again be any discrepancy between what the leaders preach and what they practice.

The old woman drew close to me, and said: "Hermas, you bear a grudge against your family. You resent your children for their bad behavior, and you resent your wife for not being more strict with them. In addition you resent your sister for the many demands she makes on you. This resentment is choking your soul, like a weed choking a fine plant, and you must root it out. It is you, not your wife, who is the cause of your children's bad behavior, because it is you, not your wife, who is failing to exert discipline. You have not been condemned by God, because in your personal life you show honesty, simplicity, and self-control. These qualities save you, and give hope for the future. Now through prayer you must find inner strength and courage, that you can fulfill your duties toward your family. You may reply that family duties are unimportant when believers all over the world are facing cruel persecution; you think that the ability to retain the faith in the face of torture and death is all that matters. But, even in these times, the crown of martyrdom is given only to a few privileged souls. For most people it is within the home and among neighbors that they must learn to participate in the death and new life of the Lord."

The old woman paused, and then she spoke again: "Hermas, you are guilty of pride. You are proud because you are brave in the face of persecution. In your heart you congratulate yourself for remaining true to your faith, in the midst of great danger. You look down on those who have denied their faith rather than risk torture and death. You think you are an example which others should follow. As you are hearing me speak, in your mind you are indignantly denying my accusation. Your mind is indeed innocent; you would not allow any proud thoughts into your mind. The pride lies hidden in your heart, where you can ignore it. You have learned to think humbly about yourself, but not to feel humbly. As a result your heart is being destroyed. Look into your heart for this poison of pride, and through prayer and fasting purify your heart. Then your emotions and your thoughts will work together, and both will belong to God."

The old woman left me. Then a beautiful young man appeared. "Who do you think that woman was who gave you the book?" he asked me. I replied that I had no idea. The young man smiled and said nothing. So I pressed him: "Who was she?" "The Church," he replied. "Why is she so old when the Church is still young?" "The Church is not young," the man replied, "it is as old as creation itself." I was baffled, and asked: "How can the Church be so old? Jesus of Nazareth created the Church, and there are some alive today who saw him in the flesh." "Jesus of Nazareth established the visible Church," the man replied, "but the Word of God established the invisible Church." "And who belongs to this invisible Church?" I asked. "All who can discern the Word of God in the beauty and harmony of God's creation," he said, "and all who can discern the Word of God in the beauty and harmony of the human soul. There have been men and women since the earliest days who have possessed such discernment; and they have been saved."

thought deeply about what the young man said. Then I asked him: "If there has always been an invisible Church, why did Jesus establish a visible Church?" "God decided," the young man replied, "that the time had come to reveal his secret purpose. So the Word of God became flesh in the person of Jesus Christ of Nazareth; and Jesus established a visible Church to proclaim God's purpose to all mankind." "Why do people persecute the Church?" I asked. "They first persecuted Jesus himself. The divine goodness of his life and words showed to people the evil and wickedness of their lives and words. Some repented and became his disciples. But others refused to repent, and preferred instead to destroy him. Now that Jesus has returned to heaven, the Church is his visible body on earth. The divine goodness of the Church's life and works must show by comparison the evil of this world. In every generation some will repent and join the Church, while others will refuse to repent and seek to destroy the Church."

he young man now left me, and I awoke. I slowly walked home, thinking about what the young man had said, and about the message which I had copied from the book. The message of the book is that the Church is failing to be the visible body of Christ on earth, because its leaders are full of pride, greed, and hypocrisy. I wondered if people would soon stop persecuting the Church, and instead become indifferent to her. I also wondered if people would stop repenting, so that within one or two generations the Church would disappear. Then I began to feel frightened that the leaders would punish me when I conveyed to them the message of the book. Finally, I reached home, and fell asleep on my bed. While I slept, the old woman returned. I begged her to spare me the duty of delivering the message to the Church leaders. She bent over me and stroked my head. When I awoke I was filled with courage, and knew that, if I spoke the message with confidence, the Church leaders would not dare to punish me, but would take heed of what I said.

I now fasted for eight days and nights. On the last night of my fast, the old woman came to me again. She ordered me to go out into the fields where I was growing crops. "Which field?" I asked her. "You can choose," she replied. So I went to a quiet secluded spot, where I waited for many hours. Then I saw nearby a couch made of ivory, with a linen sheet spread over it, and at one end a linen pillow. The sight of this couch filled me with fear and my hair stood on end; and as I was alone I began to panic. After a few moments I took control of my wits by reminding myself of God's mercy. Then the old woman arrived with six young men, and she told me to confess my sins. I spoke at great length, telling her in detail about every sin I could remember. My memory took me back to my early childhood, and I told her how at times I disobeyed my parents, even on one occasion stealing some coins from my father. I told of sexual sins I committed before my conversion. Every sin I recalled reminded me of another sin, and so I continued to speak for many hours. Tears of shame were soon flowing from my eyes, and my heart felt as if it would soon burst with grief.

s I confessed my sins I was kneeling, with my forehead touching the ground. Finally after many hours, she leaned down and lifted me by the shoulders. "Your eyes are red and swollen," she said, "and your cheeks have been streaked by tears rolling down them. Your whole body is wet with perspiration. You are in agony, and yet you are joyful." I looked up at her face. No words came from my lips, but she could see that I was baffled by what she had said. "Yes, dear Hermas, you have enjoyed speaking about your sins. Your confession has been true and sincere; and for that reason God will forgive you. Yet you have been wallowing in your sins. You derive pleasure in talking about yourself. Even as you abase yourself, pride is infecting your heart. If there were no pride, you would be impatient to get up and take care of your family whom you have cruelly neglected. You are using strict religious observance as a means of avoiding your duties." Then she took me by the hand, and led me to the ivory couch.

When the old woman and I reached the ivory couch, she sat in the middle, and she beckoned me to sit on her left. I asked her why I should sit on her left and not on her right. "Are you upset that I require you to sit on my left?" she asked. I blushed, but did not reply. "Yes," she said, "I see you are upset. How silly you are! What does it matter whether you sit on my left or my right?" "Everything you do has a reason," I replied, "and I believe that your right-hand side is the place of highest honor." "Yes, you are correct," she said with a gentle smile. "I can see into the hearts of people, and I know every pleasure they have enjoyed and every pain they have endured. I can witness the choices which people make, and I can discern the motives that lie behind those choices. To me no corner of the human heart is dark; the light of my eye shines everywhere. According to what I see and know, I beckon some to my right, and some to my left; and some I refuse to beckon, because I will not have people on my ivory couch who have not repented."

18

I asked the old woman to explain the difference between those whom she beckoned to her right side, and those whom she beckoned to her left. "Those on my right are people who have suffered for God," she replied. And she told me that I fell far short of them. I began to weep, and she put her arm around my shoulder. "Do not cry," she said softly, "because one day you shall sit on my right. You must be totally honest in your words and your actions, and that honesty will eventually make you worthy to sit on my right." I looked perplexed, because I could not understand how honesty would cause me to suffer for God. She explained that a man who is always honest about his faith will be insulted, whipped, imprisoned, and even murdered. I felt frightened because I did not know whether I had the courage to face such a fate. "Do not be afraid," she said, "because if you are always honest, God will give you the courage to endure even the most terrible suffering."

The old woman bent down and lifted from the ground a glittering rod which she pointed toward a lake. In the middle of the lake, the six young men who had come with her were building a tower made of shining stones. Thousands of men were coming across the lake in boats laden with the stones, which the young men laid one on top of the other. The stones fitted together so perfectly that no mortar was needed, and the joints were invisible, so the tower looked as though it were built of a single stone. But then I noticed that the young men rejected some stones because they were rotten or cracked or too short, and they threw them aside. When she had shown me the tower, she got up from the ivory couch to go away. But I begged her to stay. "What should I learn from the sight of the tower?" I asked. "You are a very persistent man, wanting to know everything," she replied. "Yes," I said, "I want to join the brethren who sit on your right side, and so I want to know everything which they know." "You may know lots of things," she answered, "but you may not understand them or live by them." I pleaded with her to explain the tower to me, promising that I would try to understand its meaning, and then live by what I had understood. So she began to explain it.

The tower which you see being built is me, the Church," the old woman began. "It is built on the water because your life was saved through the water of baptism by which you entered the Church; and it shall be saved by the water of the Lord's teaching which flows through the world. The six young men are the great angels of God, whose task is to build the Church and to rule the whole of creation. Those bringing the stones are the lesser angels of God, whose task is to assist the six great angels. The stones which the angels lay are the apostles and teachers and pastors and leaders who follow the way of the Lord. They fit perfectly because those apostles and other ministers who follow the Lord listen to one another carefully, and thus work in perfect harmony. But look more carefully at the stones that are being used. Not all are being brought on boats. Some are being brought up from beneath the water; these are the ones who have suffered for the Lord. And some, which have not been cut into shape, are being brought on simple rafts. These are the ones who have never known the Lord by name, but have followed faithfully the love of God in their hearts. Despite their roughness they still fit perfectly."

The old woman stopped talking, and again got up as if she were leaving. I begged her to continue, asking her what the stones that were being cast aside represented. She slowly sat down again, and said: "Look carefully at what is happening to those stones." I looked, and I saw that, while some were sinking into the waters, others lay on dry land at the base of the tower. "Those which are cast into the water are the sinners who do not repent," she said. "The ones which have cracks are those who have malice in their hearts. The ones which are rotten are those who know the truth, but do not abide by it. The ones which are too short are those who know the truth, and make some small effort to abide by it, but are lazy in their faith, and when tested quickly abandon the truth. Those stones which land at the base of the tower are sinners who wish to repent, but have not yet found the strength to do so. Some will fail to repent, and they will slip into the water. Others will succeed, and they will be lifted up and laid on the tower." I also noticed some round stones which, although they were beautifully carved, did not fit in the tower. "Those round stones," she said, "are the people who have faith, but are more concerned with the riches and pleasures of this world."

The old woman sat back, resting herself on the linen pillow. She looked weary. Then after a few moments she sat up again, and asked me: "Would you like to see something else?" I was eager to see whatever she would show. She smiled at me, and then pointed back toward the tower. "Do you see seven women around the tower?" "Yes," I said. "The tower is being supported by them. The first who is clasping her hands is called Faith. Through her, people are saved. The second, who is sturdy and tall like a man, is called Self-control; she is the daughter of Faith. Whoever follows her in this life will enjoy contentment and tranquillity of soul." "Who are the others?" I asked. "They are the daughters of one another, and they are Simplicity, Knowledge, Innocence, Reverence, and Love." I asked her how I could learn to follow these seven women. "Choose the woman whom you find most attractive," she replied. "If you follow her loyally, then you will discover how to follow all the rest. If, for example, you follow Simplicity, then you will grow in knowledge. If you follow Innocence, then you will treat other people with reverence and love. If you follow Faith, then you will acquire self-control."

The old woman now gave me a message to take to the churches across the world. "Listen to me, my children," she began. "I brought you up in great simplicity, innocence, and reverence, and I instilled righteousness into your hearts. But you prefer the ways of wickedness, and as a result there is conflict and division among you. I instruct you to be at peace with one another, to help one another in your daily work, and to share your wealth, so that those who are poor in this world's goods receive from those who are rich. Some of you are becoming ill from overeating, while others are wasting away from lack of food. This failure to share food destroys the souls of the rich and the bodies of the poor. While this injustice continues, the tower, which is the holy Church, cannot be completed. And there is a further injustice which you must root out. Your leaders enjoy great respect and status, and treat those in their charge, especially the poor and the uneducated, as if they were slaves. All are equal in the eyes of God, and those who regard themselves as superior are not fit to be leaders. Many of you are wise, but none of you is pure. Only when wisdom is mixed with purity shall you be fit to stand before your Father in heaven."

hen the old woman stopped speaking, the six young men who were building the tower came and led her away; and four others carried the ivory couch. They took the woman and the couch toward the tower. As she left I begged her to stop for a moment and explain the three forms in which she had appeared to me. "When I first saw you," I said, "you were very old, sitting on a chair and looking sad. The second time your face was younger, but your body and hair were old; you were standing up, and you looked very joyful. On this third occasion your face and your body are young and beautiful, but your hair shows you to be old; you have been sitting on a couch, and look neither joyful nor sad." She did not answer my question, but said: "Every request needs humility; so fast, and then you shall receive an answer." I fasted for a day, and that night a young man appeared to me. "Why," he asked, "do you ask constantly for revelations? Be careful, because too many revelations can injure your mind and body. You have already received enough revelations." I felt hurt and sad. "Sir," I replied, "I only ask for one more revelation, to understand the three forms of the old woman." He looked angry, and said: "Why do you persist in your foolishness? It is your stubborn pride which demands constant revelations. You imagine yourself to be spiritually superior to others, and so entitled to special revelations." "I will be humble," I answered, "if you answer this final request."

The young man agreed to explain to me the forms in which the old woman appeared. "In the first vision," he began, "she was old and seated on a chair, because your spirit is old and already fading away. Your spirit is old, not in years, but through your pride and hypocrisy which corrupt and age you from within. You have also weakened yourself through worries about wealth and work, rather than putting your trust in the Lord. She sat in a chair because an old, sick person has no strength to stand; in the same way your spirit is now too old and sick to survive on its own. In this second vision she was younger and more joyful in her form because your spirit had found new hope. Like a sad, worried person who receives an unexpected inheritance and suddenly his worries are gone, you have received the inheritance of salvation, left to you by the Lord when he died on the cross. At such a time weakness turns to strength; so she was standing. In the third vision she still had the wisdom of age, so the hair on her head was old; but in every other way she was young. Her spiritual security was shown by the ivory couch on which she sat, and her inner serenity shown by her face which was neither joyful nor sad. If you hold fast to your faith, you shall become spiritually beautiful, yet also wise; and you shall feel secure in God's love, and hence serene and tranquil." Then the young man disappeared and I awoke; and so my third vision ended.

The fourth vision came to me twenty days after the third vision, and it concerned the coming persecution. I was walking into the country on the Via Campana. I left the public road, and walked about a mile to a remote spot, where I begged the Lord to complete the revelations he was giving to me, and to give me the strength to convey his message to the Church. While I was praying I heard a voice, which seemed to be an echo of my own. "Do not be impatient, Hermas," the voice said. The voice went silent for a while, and I wondered in what way I was being impatient. Then the voice spoke again: "You are frightened of the coming persecution, and yet you are impatient for it. You are frightened of giving the message to the Church, and yet you are impatient for it. You actually want to suffer persecution and win the crown of martyrdom. And before the persecution, you want to be hailed by the Church as a great prophet. The man who courts martyrdom is no martyr. The speaker who wants to be God's mouthpiece has nothing to say. The person who desires martyrdom and desires the gift of prophecy is infected by pride. Only a person without pride is fit to speak for the Lord and die for the Lord."

continued to pray, and again I heard a voice which seemed to be an echo of my own. "Do not be two-minded, Hermas," the voice said. I wondered in what ways I was two-minded; I believed that the Lord himself had given me such a firm foundation in faith that my mind was wholly occupied with spiritual things. I walked a little further along the road. Then I saw dust rising from the ground a short distance away. I wondered if cattle were coming toward me and raising the dust. But the cloud of dust grew larger and larger, and reached higher and higher toward the sky. Then I saw a great beast like a Leviathan, and fiery locusts were coming out of its mouth. The beast was about thirty yards long, and its head was like a piece of pottery. I began to weep and pray to the Lord to save me from it; and as I prayed I remembered the words, "Do not be two-minded, Hermas." Then I took courage and faced the beast. It rushed toward me, but when it came near it lay down on the ground with its tongue out, and did not move till I had passed by. It had on its head four colors: black, red, gold, and white.

After I had passed the beast and had gone about ten yards further, a young woman appeared, dressed as if for a wedding, with white clothes and sandals, a veil over her face, and a turban on her head. I recognized her as the same person as the old woman I had seen in earlier visions, who represented the Church. I was filled with joy at her pure beauty. She greeted me warmly. I told her about the great beast I had just encountered, and how by the Lord's mercy I had escaped it. "You escaped it," she said, "because you put your trust in the Lord, so he sent his angel to protect you. You were saved from great suffering by not being two-minded when you saw the beast. That beast represents the persecution that is coming to the Church. Go back, therefore, and tell the Church about the Lord's great mercy. Instruct people to prepare for the persecution by repenting with all their hearts, and thus ensuring that their hearts remain pure and blameless. Let them not be two-minded, sometimes trusting in their own strength and sometimes trusting in the Lord's strength. If they wish to be saved, they must trust only in the Lord. If their faith fails, it would be better for them never to have been born."

I asked the woman about the four colors which the beast had on its head. "Black is the world," she said, "in which you are living. Red means that this world must be destroyed by fire and blood. Gold is you, because you will be refined in the fire and be made pure. Gold is also the others who will be refined in the fire. And then you and all those people will be used in building the Church. White is the world to come, in which those who have been made spotless and pure will dwell." I felt frightened at the prospect of the great suffering which her words foretold; for, although I wished to be pure, I dreaded the refining fire of persecution. She leaned toward me, and the closeness of her beautiful young face comforted me and gave me courage. "In the period before the fire and the blood," she said, "you must seize every opportunity to speak to the Church, and urge the people to repent. If you have the courage to speak, even when people are hostile and angry at your words, you will have courage to endure the coming persecution." Then a cloud descended over her; and when the cloud lifted she had gone. I walked home trembling, because at each step I wondered if the beast would attack me.

30

While I was sitting on my bed at home, praying to the Lord, a wonderfully handsome man appeared. He was dressed as a shepherd, with a white coat made of goatskin, a bag over his shoulders, and a staff in his hands. He sat down beside me on the bed, and said: "I am your companion, the closest friend you have, sent by the Lord." I thought at first he was deceiving me; I wondered if he were a thief or even a murderer, so I shook with fear. "Do not be afraid," the man said, "I have been with you since you were born." "But I have never seen you before," I said. "You have not seen me," he replied, "because you have not been ready to see me. Every person that is born into the world has a companion sent by the Lord." His voice seemed strangely familiar; and I realized it was just like my own, but clearer and stronger. And his features seemed familiar also; and I realized his face was just like my own, but more radiant and joyful. "I am you," the man said, "as God wants you to become. When you become like me, I will leave you."

looked intently at the man dressed as a shepherd, who was sitting on my bed. "Why has the Lord chosen to reveal you to me now?" I asked. "It is because your ears are now open to hear deep truths, and your eyes are now open to see deep mysteries. You feel weak, but I will give you strength. You feel foolish, but I will give you wisdom. My purpose is to instruct you in all the matters which you already know in your heart. I will give you commandments, and I will unfold parables. Although you are illiterate, you will be able to write down what you hear and see; the Lord himself will move your hand across the page. You must keep all the commandments, repenting your past sin, and remaining from now onward pure and blameless. Then you shall receive the reward which the Lord has promised. But if you do not keep the commandments, you shall receive the opposite of a reward." Then the shepherd began to dictate the commandments, and I wrote them down.

First, believe that God is one. Divine power is all around you. It is God who makes the corn grow, and the trees come into leaf each spring. It is God who makes the fish swim and the deer leap. It is God who causes people to laugh and cry, to sing and dance. God manifests his power in an infinite number of different ways; he reveals himself in an infinite number of different forms. So sometimes people think there are many gods, one god for each sign of divine power. But there is only one God. He created all things, and is himself uncreated. He contains all things, and is himself uncontained. He sustains all things, and himself needs no sustenance. He will perfect all things, and is himself perfect. Believe in him and fear him; and let fear bring self-control, so you shall cast off the garments of wickedness, and dress yourself in righteousness.

Second, be as simple and innocent as a little child. Do not try even to understand how evil minds and hearts work, because if you understand you will be tempted to imitate. Do not fill your head with complex theories about God and the heavens, because no human ideas can penetrate the divine mystery; God has revealed enough of himself for each of us to love him with all our hearts. Speak evil of no one, and do not listen to those who speak evil of others. If you listen to those speaking evil, you share in their sin, and you find yourself believing what they say. Do not respect the rank or status of others, but treat all as equals. Give generously and without hesitation when you see others in need, because God wants his gifts to you to be turned into gifts from you to others. Do not keep an account of what you have given, and leave it to others to give an account to God of what they have received from you. When you yourself need the kindness of others, receive their gifts with gratitude; but, just as you are not superior to those to whom you give help, do not feel inferior to those from whom you receive help.

Third, love truth. Let all the words that come from your mouth be truthful. In this way your own heart will become truthful, and the spirit of the Lord will be able to dwell there. Those who tell lies are not only defrauding those to whom they speak, but they are defrauding themselves and God. Each person is offered by God the spirit of truth; and those who lie are throwing that gift back to him. There are many merchants and other businesspeople who think that lies and fraud will bring them prosperity; and they seek to compensate for those lies by being honest in matters unconnected with business. Those who wish the spirit of God to dwell in their hearts must be honest at all times and in all circumstances, and God will cause the honest businessperson to prosper accordingly. Yet there are some who are gripped by an evil conscience, imagining themselves to be liars and cheats, when in fact they are honest with themselves, with others, and with God. It is for each person to look very carefully at himself, to assess whether he is honest or false. And if he is honest, he should ask God to give him a peaceful and a tranquil heart.

ourth, keep your minds free of any impure thoughts. Many imagine that only deeds can be sinful, and that thoughts escape judgment. But it is evil thinking that causes evil action; so sin must be rooted out of the mind, if our deeds are to be righteous. A man must not desire another man's wife, and a woman must not desire another woman's husband. If one partner commits adultery, and later truly repents, then the other partner must remain faithful. But if a partner commits adultery and does not repent, then the other partner would become a participant in the sin by preserving the marriage. When a husband or wife commits adultery and does not repent, the other partner should leave the marriage and live alone. The way to avoid adulterous or any other kind of evil thought is to open your heart to the Holy Spirit and allow the Spirit to fill your heart with divine joy. The pleasures of the flesh will seem trivial, and temptation will melt away. A person who has once known the joy of God will never want to jeopardize it by entertaining evil thoughts, even for a second.

ifth, be courageous and yet prudent, and you will always do what is right. If you are courageous the Holy Spirit, who dwells within you, will be pure, not obscured by the evil spirit of fear. Courage enables us to seize the opportunities for righteousness which God provides, while fear causes us to draw back. God will always reward acts of courage, so we need not be frightened of any danger. Fear oppresses the soul and chokes all good intentions; the person filled with fear knows what is right, but fails to act. The root of fear is distrust in God's providence; courage comes from trust in God. Fear and courage cannot live together. If you take a little wormwood and pour it into a jar of honey, the whole jar is spoiled; a very great quantity of honey can be ruined by very little wormwood, taking away its sweetness. In the same way a small degree of fear can undermine courage. Yet courage must be tempered with prudence, so that courage does not turn into impetuosity. Consider carefully each opportunity as it arises, praying for God's guidance on how to act; and when in prudence you have decided what is right, act decisively.

Sixth, control your temper so that it is directed only to what is good and right. Ill temper can destroy even the best of actions. It enters the hearts of people, making them feel bitter about even the most trivial matters; and it destroys friendship, by turning small mishaps into causes of deep resentment. Ill temper starts with foolishness: a person responds excessively to some incident. From foolishness comes bitterness, from bitterness comes wrath, from wrath comes rage, from rage comes fury; and fury leads to the most terrible sins, including even murder. The person who is prone to ill temper is dragged in all directions, from one cruel act to another. Yet the same quality of passion, which can lead to ill temper, can also engender the most wonderful acts of righteousness. The heart, with a burning passion for righteousness, can defy and destroy every evil in this world. The person of righteous passion is always gentle and kind with those who are weak and vulnerable, because this anger is directed toward those who oppress them. And far from being the enemy of peace, the passion of righteousness ultimately brings harmony in relationships between people and tranquillity within the soul.

Seventh, always keep faith. The person who keeps faith walks on a smooth, straight road, whereas the person without faith follows a rough, crooked path, with many rocks in the way and thorn bushes on all sides. Without faith a person has no sense of direction and purpose in his actions, because he does not have God to lead him. Small problems become large obstacles because he does not have God's Spirit to help him overcome them. And trivial difficulties become causes of great irritation and upset, because he cannot see any reason to endure them. But the person with faith knows that God is leading him through life, straight toward the joys of heaven. Problems seem to disappear as he approaches them, because the Spirit lifts him over them. And he is willing to endure great suffering, because the joy of God fills his soul, and the hope of heaven spurs him on. Keep faith by seeking God's guidance in every circumstance and at every moment, praying to him for all things.

ighth, fear the Lord, and keep his commandments. If you resolutely follow the commandments of God, you will be strong in all you do. By fearing God you will be resolute, and so you will do all things well. Fear of God will give you power over evil, because your fear of incurring God's wrath by sinning will be far greater than the greatest temptation. Where there is no fear, there is no strength. Those without fear of God pursue whatever sinful whim enters their hearts, because they are indifferent to the consequences of sin. They thus become the playthings of the evil spirits of the world. In truth there are two sorts of fear that you should have. The first sort is fear of God, which comes from a recognition of God's almighty power and majesty. The second is fear of the devil, which comes from a recognition of the devil's subtle and devious tricks. If you fear the devil, you will want to avoid contact with any kind of evil deed or person, for fear that the devil will lure you into his trap. If you fear God, you will know that by following his commandments he will ensure, by his mighty power, that all will go well with you.

In the ninth place, show temperance. Temperance is twofold: from some things you should refrain, and from some you should not. Refrain from evil, but do not refrain from good. Sometimes people refrain from doing good, because they are frightened that others might disagree with their actions and condemn them; much good is left undone owing to peoples' fear of conflict. Refrain from self-indulgence, such as excessive eating and drunkenness. Refrain from being haughty toward others, treating them as inferior to yourself, and refrain from boasting about your abilities or wealth, making others feel inferior; remember that in God's eyes all people are equal, and that abilities and wealth are gifts from God. Refrain from hypocrisy, in which you seek to give others the impression of great virtue; it is virtue itself, not the good opinion of others, that a person should pursue. Refrain from all kinds of lying, because even a lie spoken with good intentions gives birth to other lies, which destroy trust and harmony. But do not refrain from helping the destitute, nor from helping widows and orphans. Do not refrain from welcoming strangers into your home. Do not refrain from seeking peace where there is conflict. Do not refrain from intervening when people are being oppressed or cheated, but stand up for justice. Do not refrain from reproving sinners, because to allow a sin to be committed without reproach is to collude with that sin. Do not refrain from any opportunity to tell others about the faith within you.

In the tenth place, ensure that you are not two-minded or hypocritical. There are many who commit acts of malice, while pretending to others, and even to themselves, that their deeds are righteous. There are many who portray themselves as merciful, but all the while are looking for opportunities to take revenge on their enemies. There are many who appear to be peacemakers, but try to destroy their enemies by means that cannot be detected. There are many who are devout in their religion, but are indifferent to God's commandments at home or at work. There are many who will only act righteously when others are watching, but will be mean and hardhearted when no one can see. You must be indifferent to the opinion of others, and concern yourself only with God's opinion, because he alone can see every action and every thought. If you are single-minded in trying to please God, then the temptation to act hypocritically will melt away, and your outward appearance will reflect precisely your inner intentions.

In the eleventh place, be joyful. God wants you to be joyful; and if you truly dedicate yourself to God, he will bestow upon you the gift of joy. The joyful person takes pleasure in good deeds and good thoughts, and shuns evil deeds and thoughts. But the person who is caught up in bitterness and resentment finds solace in evil thoughts and deeds. Joyful persons want to pray, because they take pleasure in the presence of God; and hour by hour they intercede for others. But those whose hearts are joyless are indifferent to the presence of God, and so have no desire to pray for others. Misery is like a weight that oppresses the soul; it is like vinegar which, mixed with wine, turns that which is sweet into something unpleasant. There are times when it is natural for a person to be sad, and such sadness purifies the soul. But constant sadness is a form of self-indulgence, perverting the soul by turning a person's thoughts into himself.

In the twelfth place, put away from yourself all evil desire, and put on yourself only desires which are good and holy. Good desire curbs evil desire. Left to itself, evil desire runs wild within the soul, devouring all that is good and holy, and poisoning every thought and feeling. But the person who seeks to assess every desire, determining which is good and which is evil, and then deliberately accepts the good and rejects the evil, finds that goodness is stronger than evil. The wild beast of evil will be tamed, the poison in its bite neutralized, and goodness can rule the heart. If you find yourself desiring your neighbor's spouse, then curb that desire at once by fostering the desire for your own spouse and for God himself. If you find yourself desiring another person's wealth, curb that desire by nurturing within yourself gratitude for what you yourself possess. If you find yourself desiring another person's downfall, and you begin scheming against that person, curb that desire by wishing good for that person, and thinking about ways to serve him. There will at first, in every case, be a battle between evil and good desires; but in God's strength the good will triumph.

Keep all these commandments not out of duty or fear, but out of desire. The commandments of God may appear like heavy burdens to carry, that will crush all life and energy from your soul. And so they are to those who do not wish to obey them. Indeed there are many people who struggle to obey God's commandments only because they are frightened of the punishment he metes out to sinners. But such fear is only the beginning of faith; true faith is founded on love, which banishes all fear. If you love God, his commandments become your desire, his will becomes your wish. Far from feeling crushed, your heart and soul will be light; God's Spirit will seem to dance inside you. Far from losing all energy, you will be filled with zeal, enthusiastic for every task which God may give you. So look inside your heart and find that spark of love; then fan it until it glows and roars. Let the fire of divine love blaze within you.

The young shepherd paused, and looked at me intently. I felt overawed by what he had said, but I knew he had spoken rightly. "If you keep these commandments," he said, "then you will be a true and perfect servant of God. But your task is not only to keep the commandments yourself, but to exhort others to do so. You must urge people to repent of their sins, and purify themselves according to the instructions I have given. When you speak, you will win the friendship and love of those whose hearts are ready to repent, and they will obey your words." "Sir," I replied, "the commandments you have given are great and beautiful and glorious; and those who were able to keep them would truly be blessed. But the commandments are very hard, and I do not know whether ordinary mortals are able to keep them." His face became angry and his voice rose. "If you are determined to keep these commandments," he said, "then you will succeed quite easily. But if you doubt your own ability to keep them, then you will fail. But I say to you, if you do not keep these commandments, and instead ignore them, you will not be saved. It is not God who will have guided you; you will have passed judgment on yourself and condemned yourself to everlasting misery."

46

The shepherd's anger confused and upset me. I honestly did not believe I had the spiritual strength to keep the commandments he had given; and if I could not succeed, then it would be hypocritical of me to urge others to keep the commandments. When the shepherd saw my confusion, his face softened and his voice became kinder and more gentle. "You foolish and ignorant man," he said, "you do not understand the great glory of God, nor his power and majesty. It was he who created the world, and appointed human beings to be masters of his creation. Thus, if human beings are the master of all the creatures under heaven, surely they can master these commandments. Those who have the Lord in their heart can certainly master these commandments. Yet those who have the Lord on their lips, but not in their hearts, will find these commandments impossible to master. So let the Lord enter your heart, and you will find that nothing is sweeter or more gentle than these commandments. But if you keep the Lord out of your heart not only will you fail to keep these commandments but also you will plunge into misery and bitterness because the devil will take command of you."

ir," I said to the shepherd, "will you please listen to a few words from me?" "Say what you like," the shepherd replied. "A man may desire to keep the commandments of God," I said, "and he may pray most earnestly to God for the strength to keep them. With all his heart he may wish to submit to God. But the devil is sly and cunning, and constantly causes him to trip and fall."

"The devil," answered the shepherd, "cannot win against a heart that is truly devoted to the Lord. The devil will wrestle with such a heart, and may at times seem to enjoy the upper hand. But the heart that trusts in God's power will always resist and defeat the devil, and the devil will fly away in shame. Let me illustrate what I mean. A person pours good wine into jars. Most of the jars are filled to the brim, but in some are put only half the amount of wine that they can hold. The wine in the full jars will remain sweet and pleasant, but the wine in the half-empty jars will go sour. In the same way a heart filled with the love of God will have no room for the devil to enter. But a heart only half filled with the love of God leaves empty room for the devil to enter and turn the heart sour and bad."

There is an angel of repentance," the shepherd continued, "who is with all people who wish to repent of their sins. This angel gives them strength, so that they can see their sins for what they are, and then turn away from those sins. This angel brings faith, so that repentant sinners are directed toward God, and their feet are set firmly on the road to heaven. And the angel brings solace, so the grief at giving up sin is overcome by the pleasure of God's love. When a person truly repents, it is like a great load being lifted from his shoulders; he feels free and his steps become light." "Sir," I replied, "I believe that you yourself are that angel, and you will give me the strength to keep God's commandments. With you I shall break the power of the devil, and he will become as powerless to harm me as the muscles of a dead body. And with you I shall find the courage and determination to walk always on the path of God, never deviating from the smooth, straight road that leads to heaven." The shepherd embraced me, and said: "Yes, you shall succeed. Your brave words shall be fulfilled, and you shall live for God alone."

The shepherd now began to speak in parables. "As servants of God," he began, "you are strangers in the world, because you belong to the heavenly kingdom. Your city is far from this city. So, then, if you know the city in which you are going to dwell, why do you devote yourselves to constructing luxurious homes here in this city? Those who devote themselves to their own personal well-being in this city will not be able to enter the heavenly city. Foolish and miserable ones, do you not understand that the things of this city are foreign to you, and you are under the power of another? The lord of the earthly city will say: 'I do not want you to dwell here, because you do not conform to our laws; you belong elsewhere.' Thus your faith in God makes you unwelcome in the world. And the Lord of the heavenly city will say: 'I do not want you to dwell here, because you do not conform to our laws; you belong elsewhere.' Thus the fields and mansions and the many other possessions you have acquired on earth will bar your way to heaven. If God had not called you to the heavenly city, then you would be free to follow the laws of the earthly city; this would not bring you peace or joy, but you would not be guilty, and the earthly city would be your home. But since God has called you to the heavenly city, failure to answer that call makes you not only unhappy, but also homeless."

While I was walking in the country I noticed an elm with a vine growing up it. I was thinking about the vine and the elm, and observing them closely, when the shepherd appeared to me. "What are you thinking about as you look at the elm and the vine?" he asked. "I am thinking that they are well-suited to each other," I replied. "They are symbols for the poor and the rich," he said. I asked him to explain further. "This vine," he said, "bears fruit, but the elm is a sterile tree. But the vine, if it did not cling to the elm, would fall to the ground, and its fruit would become rotten. When, therefore, it is attached to the elm, it bears fruit both from itself and from the elm. In the same way the rich people, who have much worldly wealth, are spiritually sterile, because their minds and hearts are absorbed in worldly affairs and have little time for prayer and confession. But those who are poor have no worldly affairs to absorb their hearts and minds and have ample time for prayer and confession. Left to themselves, the poor go hungry, and their hearts fill with resentment and bitterness at their condition. But if they can cling to the rich, receiving food and shelter for their body, then the poor can bear spiritual fruit for both themselves and the rich."

The shepherd showed me many trees without leaves, and the trees appeared to be all alike. "Do you see these trees?" he asked. "Yes, sir," I replied, "they seem to be all alike." "These trees," he went on, "are those who dwell in the world." I looked puzzled, and asked him why all who dwell in the world should be alike. "Because," he replied, "in this world it is not apparent who is righteous and who is sinful, but all look alike. For the righteous this world is winter, so they do not bear leaves; their leaves will sprout in the next world, which for the righteous is summer. For the sinful this world is indeed summer; but because their hearts are cold, they can bear no leaves and remain barren." I felt very sad at this parable. "Does this mean that there are no signs of true life in this world?" I asked. "When you yourself become righteous," he replied, "you will see things differently. As you gaze on the trees of the righteous, you will see in your eyes the heavenly leaves that are to come. And even on this earth those trees will look wonderfully beautiful."

52

I was sitting on a mountain, fasting and praying, when the shepherd appeared at my side. "What are you doing here?" the shepherd asked. "I am fasting, sir," I replied. "And why are you fasting?" "I am fasting, sir, because it is my custom to fast at this time." "You do not know how to fast," the shepherd said, "and so this fast is utterly useless, and is not a fast at all." "Why do you say this?" I asked. "Let me teach you about true fasting, which is acceptable and pleasing to the Lord." I said that I was eager to learn. "If you fast simply by giving up food, or abstaining from certain foods," he continued, "the Lord is completely indifferent to your efforts. The only fast which he wants is for you to abstain from all evil acts, to give up every form of evil desire, and let your heart become pure. So the person who once was malicious and schemed against others, but gives up all malice and scheming, is making a true fast. The person who once was jealous and wanted the possessions of others but gives up jealousy and is content with what the Lord provides is making a true fast. Come down from your high mountain, and make your fast among people."

I will tell you a parable which concerns fasting," the shepherd said. "A certain man had a field and many servants, and in one part of the field he planted a vineyard. He picked out a particular servant, who was loyal and honest, and told him to put a fence round it, but do nothing more to the vineyard; and he promised to give the servant his freedom if the task was done well. Then the master went away on a long journey. When the master had gone, the servant put a fence round the vineyard. But after he had finished, he noticed the vineyard was full of weeds. So he dug the vineyard and pulled out the weeds. The vineyard was now very beautiful and fertile, with no weeds to choke the vines. The master returned and was very pleased with all the servant had done. So he called the servant and all his friends together; and he publicly congratulated the servant for doing the work he was ordered to do, and then doing extra work which he had not been ordered to do. And as a reward, he announced that he would make the servant his heir. To celebrate, the master decided to hold a great feast. The master sent the servant much food to prepare for the feast. But instead of keeping the food for the feast, the servant distributed it to all the other servants. And this pleased the master even more, so that he was doubly pleased to have made the servant his joint heir."

ir," I said, "I cannot understand this parable unless you explain it to me." He replied that it is the weakness of my faith that makes my mind blind to the parable's meaning. "I agree," I said, "but if you explain the parable, then my faith will grow stronger." At this he consented to explain the parable. "The field is the world," he began, "and the master is God who created the world. The vines are the people God has planted in the world, and the servant is God's Son. The fences are the holy angels whom God has sent to protect his people. The weeds which the servant pulls out of the vineyard are all the evil desires and deeds of the people. The food which the master sent for the feast represents the commandments of God; and the Son gives these commandments to all the people. The absence of the master is the time which remains before he comes to judge the world." I was astonished at this explanation, and spent many days reflecting on it. But as I reflected, a question arose in my mind, which I put to the shepherd. "Why, sir," I asked, "does the Son of God appear in the parable in the form of a servant?"

The Son of God," the shepherd said, "is in the form of a servant because he came to earth to serve all people. He did not come as a proud prince, but as a humble servant, working for the good of others. Although he had the form of a servant and acted with profound humility, he exercised great power. God planted the vineyard—that is, he created the people—but he gave it over to his Son. And his Son put up the fence—that is, he appointed the angels—to protect people. It was when the servant dug the vineyard that the Son's humility and his power were truly brought together. Only by an act of supreme humility, allowing himself to be sentenced to death as a common criminal, could the Son achieve supreme power over the forces of evil. In this way the Son became our perfect servant by becoming our Lord and master." These words of the shepherd were so deep that with my mind I could not grasp them. But in my heart I knew that what he was saying was true. "How can a man be saved whose mind is too dull to understand these truths?" I asked. "These truths are for the heart and for the soul," the shepherd replied.

I was seated in my house, reflecting on all the blessings God had bestowed on me, when the shepherd appeared in front of me. "Let us go into the country," he said, "and I will show you the shepherds of the sheep." So we went out into the country, and arrived at a large, open plain. There he showed me a young shepherd, dressed in clothes of yellow. This shepherd was feeding numerous sheep, and the sheep were plump and frisky, and they skipped around the shepherd. And the shepherd himself looked very joyful as he looked at his flock, and he ran about among his sheep. "Do you see this shepherd?" asked the shepherd who was leading me. "Yes, I see him." "He is the angel of luxury and deceit. He feeds people well with the pleasures of this world, and for a time they are happy and joyful, full of energy and vitality. The sheep that you see skipping are those who have given themselves over completely to material luxury. And the shepherd looks happy, because he is pleased at how many sheep have been deceived by him. But if you look carefully, you can see some sheep who are not skipping, but standing still while they feed. These are the people who have been corrupted, yet who have not given themselves completely to the world; for them there is hope."

The shepherd took me to another place in the plain. There I saw a huge shepherd, his face covered by a black beard, and his vast body clothed in a white goatskin. He had a bag on his shoulders, a great staff in his hands, and a whip with knots in it. He looked angry and bitter, and I shuddered with fear at the sight of him. This shepherd was receiving sheep from the young shepherd, but the sheep were no longer skipping. The huge angry shepherd threw the sheep into a great bed of thorns and thistles; and as the sheep wriggled to try and escape, their fleeces became increasingly entangled with the thorns and thistles, so that soon the sheep could barely move. Then he began to beat them with his staff and to whip them. I did not need to ask who this shepherd was. I understood him at once to be the shepherd of punishment. Thus all those who give themselves over to the luxuries of this world will eventually suffer for their greed and their selfishness. But I felt no satisfaction in watching their pain. On the contrary, I wanted their punishment to cease, and I asked if this would happen.

The sheep who are punished," the shepherd said, "do not suffer forever. They are punished according to their misdeeds. Then they are handed over to me. It is my task to instruct them in the ways of the Lord, so that they can live in true peace and joy." "But does this punishment and instruction only happen after death, or can it occur in the world?" I asked. "No," the shepherd replied, "it can happen in this life. The punishment may take many forms on earth, from various illnesses, to insults and slander. The purpose of these punishments is not to make people pay for their misdeeds, but to unsettle their attitudes and beliefs. A person who formerly gave himself to worldly pleasure finds himself cast into despair when pleasure turns to pain; and he searches for fresh attitudes and beliefs to enable him to endure the pain. It is when that search begins that the shepherd of punishment hands the person over to me, and I direct the search. The closer the person comes to true faith, the better able he is to endure pain; and when he arrives at faith, then he thanks God with all his heart for the punishment he endured."

I returned from the plain to my home, but I could find no rest or peace there. When I tried to sleep, my eyes refused to close, and I lay awake through the long hours of the night. My mind was filled with the image of that huge shepherd with the black beard, the white goatskin cloak, the staff, and the whip. I came to believe that he had come to my home with me, and was now living in my house. Then one night my eyes closed for a short period, and the shepherd who was leading me appeared. "What is troubling you?" he asked. "I beg you, sir," I said, "to command the shepherd of punishment to leave my house, because his presence here is destroying my peace." "But he is not here," the shepherd replied. I told him that I could sense his presence. "What you sense," the shepherd said, "is your own guilty conscience. That is a sign of hope. You are at a moment of choice. You do not yet deserve to be handed over to the shepherd of punishment, but you are still feeding too much on the pleasures of this world. If you choose to reject completely the shepherd of deceit, then it will seem to you that the shepherd of punishment is departing from your home."

When the shepherd had finished speaking, I felt confused. "But I do not enjoy many pleasures of this world," I protested. I explained that I fast regularly, that my meals are sparse and simple, that I do not commit adultery, and that I live in a humble home with few possessions. "I will put a question to you," he said, "that will show you the true meaning of righteousness. Compare two men. One lives in a palace, eating the finest food and surrounded by beautiful women. But his heart is warm and generous, so that all are welcome at his table, and he gives to the poor much of what he possesses; and he is kind, faithful, and considerate to his wife. The other lives in a hovel, with only bread and water to nourish him. But his heart is bitter and mean, and he has not a good word to say about anyone, including his wife. Which of these men is closer to the Lord?" "The one in the palace," I replied. "Let your simple house become such a palace," he said, "and then your home will become a place of peace and joy."

Many days later the shepherd appeared to me, and again took me out into the country. There he showed me a great willow tree, and under its cover were gathered all who were called Christian. And beside the willow tree stood an angel, beautiful and immensely tall, who kept cutting branches off the willow tree and giving them to people in the shade of the tree. When they had all received little sticks, the angel put down his pruning hook, and the tree was still sound and its branches as complete as when I first saw it. I asked the shepherd: "How can the tree remain sound when so many branches have been cut off?" "Everything will soon be made clear," he replied. The angel asked the people to give back the sticks. Some of the sticks were now dry and rotten, and the angel asked the people who had given back these sticks to stand apart. Some gave sticks that were dry, but not rotten; some gave sticks that were half dry; some sticks were half dry with cracks; some sticks were green with cracks; some were half dry and half green; some mainly green, but with dry tips; some green with buds; some green with buds bearing fruit. And each group was told to stand apart.

The angel of the Lord commanded that crowns made of palm leaves be brought. He placed crowns on the people who had given sticks that were bearing fruit, and sent them away into the tower; he also put a white cloak on them. To those who had handed him green sticks with buds, but with no fruit, he gave seals. And he also gave seals to those who had handed him green sticks, but with no buds. The angel then said to the shepherd: "I am going away, so from now on it is for you to decide who may enter the tower. When I return I will test on the altar all whom you let into the tower." When the angel had left, the shepherd said to me: "Let us take all the sticks and plant them in the ground to see which will live." "Sir," I asked, "how can these dry sticks possibly live?" "The willow is a very tenacious tree," he replied, "and it clings to life. If these sticks receive a little water they may yet live; and we shall water them. If any live, I shall rejoice. And if any die, it will not be through lack of effort on our part." So the shepherd took all the sticks and planted them in ranks; and then he poured water all around them, so the sticks could not be seen for water.

After he had watered the sticks, the shepherd said: "Let us go away for a few days, and then return to see how the sticks are faring. The one who created the tree wishes all those who received sticks from the tree to live. And I hope that, by watering them, I will have enabled the greater part of them to survive." After we had left the willow tree, I asked him how the tree remained so full and healthy after so many branches had been cut off it. "This great tree," he explained, "is God's law which has been given to all the earth. And this law is embodied in God's Son, whose words have been preached to all the earth. Those who are under its shade are those who have heard his preaching and believed in it. The angel is Michael, who has power over those people and governs them. By giving each person a stick, he is ensuring that each one has truly received God's law. He then watches over them to see if they obey God's law. The fate of each stick is determined by the degree to which the person holding that stick is obedient."

ir," I asked the shepherd, "why did the angel send some to the tower, while leaving some to you?" "All those who had obeyed the law were ready to go straight to the tower, which is God's kingdom. But those who had transgressed the law were left under my authority, so that I could encourage them to repent." "And why," I asked, "do some receive crowns?" "All those," he answered, "whose sticks had buds which were bearing fruit are those who have suffered and been persecuted for the law. Therefore they receive a crown. Those whose sticks were green with buds, but no fruit, are people who have obeyed the law, but not suffered for it. Thus they are welcomed into the tower, but do not receive a crown. Those whose sticks are green, but with no buds, are people who have had little opportunity to disobey the law, and so have not even had to endure temptation. They, too, are welcome in the tower, but have a lesser place. I will explain about the others when we return to look at the sticks which were planted in the ground and watered."

few days later we returned to the willow tree. The shepherd told me to call together the people whose sticks he had planted. Then he said to them: "Let each of you pull his own stick out of the ground and give it to me." Some of the sticks that were handed to him were exactly the same as they had been when he planted them. But some which had been dry and cracked were now green and healthy. When he had taken all the sticks, he said to me: "I told you that the tree is tenacious and clings to life. Do you see how many have repented and been saved?" "Yes, sir," I replied. "See, then," he went on, "how merciful is the Lord, because he has given his spirit of life to those who seemed dead." "Why, sir," I asked, "did not all the sticks repent?" "It depends on the nature of their sins, and how easy it is to repent," he replied. I looked perplexed, so he continued. "If their sin is overindulgence, then they themselves can see it clearly, and so repentance is easy. If their sin is adultery and fornication, the same applies. If it is malice, the same applies. But if their sin is rooted in dishonesty, lying, guile, and fraud, then they deceive themselves as well as others. They may imagine themselves righteous, even when sinning. For them, repentance is very hard."

I asked the shepherd to explain more fully the meaning of the different kinds of sticks. "The sticks that are dry and rotten belong to those who betray Christ and deny their faith when put to the test. Those whose sticks are dry, but not rotten, are people who will talk as if they believe, but whose faith has not touched their hearts. The sticks which have cracks belong to hypocrites, who make great efforts to appear virtuous to others, but in private feel no guilt about committing further sin. All these have great difficulty in repenting because they are deceitful, even toward themselves: they think they are good Christians, but in truth they have not changed. The people whose sticks are half dry and half green want to obey God's law, and often succeed in doing so, but their wills are weak, and frequently they slip back into their sinful ways. The people whose sticks are mainly green, but with a dry tip, lead good and virtuous lives; yet they lack the courage to tell others about their faith. All these can readily be persuaded to repent."

The shepherd took me to a mountain and sat me on one of its pinnacles. He then showed me a vast open plain stretching in all directions; in the plain there were twelve mountains, each the shape of a perfect cone. But the mountains were all different. The first was black as pitch. The second was bare, without anything growing on it. The third was full of thorns and thistles. The fourth was covered with herbs, of which the tops were green and the roots dry. The fifth had green herbs, but the ground was rough. The sixth was full of cracks, some wide and some narrow; the cracks had plants growing in them, but the plants were fading. The seventh was covered with lush grass, with all kinds of cattle and sheep feeding on it. The eighth had many springs gushing from it, with all sorts of creatures drinking from the springs. The ninth had no water at all and was like a desert, with deadly reptiles crawling over it. The tenth had great trees giving ample shade, and under the trees sheep were lying. The eleventh mountain was covered with fruit trees, with succulent ripe fruit hanging from every one. And the twelfth mountain was completely white.

In the middle of the plain, the shepherd showed me a great white rock, which had risen out of the plain. The rock was higher than the twelve mountains and was large enough to hold the whole world. The rock was old, and it had a gateway into it, which appeared to have been hewn recently. The gate glistened in the sun, and I marveled at its brightness. The gate had a porch, and within the porch stood twelve maidens. The four who stood at the corners seemed to me the most beautiful, but the ones standing between them were also beautiful. They were clothed in linen mantles, with their right shoulders bare as if they were about to carry a load. They looked very joyful and eager. As my eyes rested on the lovely sight, I felt perplexed, because the maidens appeared so delicate, and yet I could sense in them great courage, as if they were ready to carry the whole of heaven. Then the shepherd said to me: "Why do you trouble yourself with questions? If you cannot understand something, do not be anxious; the Lord will reveal to you what you need to know. Do not be curious about what you cannot see or understand; only try to grasp what you can see and understand."

I saw six men, tall and handsome, and all similar in appearance. They summoned a great multitude of other men, who were also tall, handsome, and strong. The six commanded them to build a tower above the rock. Soon all the men were moving busily this way and that. The maidens held out their hands as if they were about to receive something from the sky. The six men commanded stones to appear from the ground for building the tower. Then huge, square stones came up, beautiful and not hewn. The six men commanded the maidens to pick up the stones, take them through the gateway, and up to the men building the tower. The maidens put the stones together, and carried them as if they were a single stone. These stones made the foundations of the tower. Then twenty-five more stones appeared, which were laid on top of the foundations. Then came thirty-five more stones, followed by forty stones, making successive tiers of the tower. The men now rested for a while. When they were refreshed, the six men ordered the multitude to collect stones from the mountains. But these were all different colors, and looked ugly when laid on the tower. So the six men ordered them to be taken back. And they said to the multitude: "You must always hand the stones to the maidens for them to carry through the gateway and up to the tower. Unless they are brought to the tower by the maidens, they will not change color, and your labor will be in vain."

The six men ordered the multitude who were build-ing the tower to stop and rest; but they told the maidens to stay by the tower. It seemed to me that the maidens were no longer concerned about the tower. Since the tower was almost complete, I asked the shepherd why the men had not finished it before resting. "The tower," he replied, "cannot be completed unless its lord comes and tests it. If any stones prove to be rotten he will change them." "I should like to understand the meaning of all that I have seen," I said. "If it is not vain curiosity, but a real desire for truth which prompts you," he replied, "then we shall return in a few days, and you will understand its meaning perfectly." We went away, and came back a few days later. "The lord of the tower is about to examine it," the shepherd said. We went up to the tower, but only the maidens were there; and they confirmed that the lord of the tower was about to come. I felt frightened, and yet also eager to see what would happen. "Look inside your-self," the shepherd said, "because fear and curiosity are waging war inside your heart. Let fear be replaced by trust; and curiosity by zeal for truth. Then you shall become calm, and yet also alert."

71

After a little while I saw what seemed like an army of men coming; and in the middle of them was a man so tall that he was higher than the tower. I realized that the tall man was the lord of the tower. The six men, who had been in charge of building the tower, were walking with him, on his left side and on his right, and so also were the multitude of men who had done the work. The maidens ran to him and walked with him round the tower. He examined the building carefully, feeling each stone with his hand, and then hitting it with his staff. When he struck them, some became black as pitch, some crumbled, some cracked, some showed stains, and some shook because they did not fit with the other stones. He demanded that all these rotten stones be taken out of the building, to be put on the ground beside the tower, and other stones be put in their place. The tall man commanded that a particular point in the plain be quarried, and from it the most splendid stones were found, some round and some square. The square stones were put straight into the building, but the round stones were put on one side because it would take longer to hew them into the right shape.

The tall man, who was the lord of the tower, called the shepherd and gave to him all the stones which had been taken out of the building. "Clean these stones carefully," the tall man said, "and put into the building those which can fit in with the rest. But throw away far from the tower those which do not fit." The tall man now left, with all those who had been following him, and only the maidens remained to guard the tower. I asked the shepherd how these bad stones could be made suitable for the tower. "Some will need much hewing," he replied, "because they are mostly rotten, with only a little good stone in the middle. These will be so small that I will put them in the middle of the building. But others have only an outer layer of bad stone, so even after this has been cut off they will remain large. These I will put on the outside." So we began to look carefully at all the stones. Those which were black he threw away because they were completely bad. Then he began to hew those with cracks. In some, the cracks were superficial, so they could be made into good stones; but in others the cracks went right through, so they were thrown away. Some of them turned into dust as soon as the shepherd touched them; so he swept the dust away. But others had a solid core. Those with stains that were discolored right through he threw away; but in others the stains could be scraped off. And all those which shook could be quite easily cut to the right shape. The maidens took all the stones which the shepherd had made good, and fitted them into the building.

The shepherd looked at the round stones, which were pure white. "What do we do with these stones?" he asked me. "How should I know, sir?" I replied. "Do you not notice anything about them?" he asked. "Sir, I am not a stonecutter, nor do I have any deep insights." "Do you not see," he said, "that they are perfectly round? So a great deal must be cut away from them if they are to be made square and put into the building." He took the brightest of them, and hewed them into a square shape; then the maidens fitted them into the building. The rest were carried back to the plain, and put in the quarry from which they had come. The shepherd looked up at the tower, and saw that it was now complete. He cried with joy at its beauty, and I, too, was astonished at such a wonderful sight. All the stones fit together so perfectly that it appeared to have been built from a single stone. The shepherd told me to fetch some lime and clay from the plain, and he used this to make the ground around the tower perfectly level. The maidens swept and washed the ground, until it shone in the sun. The shepherd now said that he wished to leave, but I begged him to stay and explain all he had shown me. He told me to stay with the maidens for two days, and then he would return and explain everything.

The shepherd left, and the maidens ran up to me and kissed me. Then we danced and sang together like little children. When night came they put their linen tunics on the ground, and we lay down side by side. "You shall sleep with us as a brother, not as a husband," they said, "and we shall always live with you, because we love you so dearly." For those two days with the maidens I was happier than I had ever been before. Then the shepherd returned, and he and I sat together. "First of all, sir," I said, "explain to me the rock and the gate." "The rock and the gate," he replied, "are the Son of God. The rock is old because the Son of God, who was the agent of God's creation, is older than creation. The gate is new, because it is only in recent times that the Son of God has revealed the gateway into God's kingdom. You remember that the stones used for building the tower had to enter through the gate; that is because a person can only enter the kingdom of God through God's Son. The tall man who examined the tower and its stones is God's chief angel, and the six men who had charge of building the tower are his assistants."

What is the tower?" I asked the shepherd. "The tower," he said, "is the Church." "And who are the maidens?" "They," he said, "are holy spirits. A person cannot enter the kingdom of God unless they carry him in their arms. That is why they had to take all the stones through the gateway to the tower. It is the maidens that gave the stones the power to become part of the tower; it is the Holy Spirit that gives people the power to become part of the Church. It is the maidens who ensured the stones fit so perfectly that the tower appeared to have been built with a single stone; it is the Holy Spirit who ensures that all members of the Church can live in perfect harmony." "Why, then," I asked, "were some of the stones which the maidens brought through the gate, and which were fitted into the tower, eventually rejected?" "They were rejected because after they had been put into the building, they turned bad; this was shown when the tall man struck them with his staff. In the same way some people who receive the Holy Spirit and enter the Church, later reject the salvation they have been given. Such people are the greatest sinners and must be thrown out of the Church."

Tell me, sir," I asked, "the names of the maidens."
"The four stronger maidens," the shepherd replied,
"who stand at the four corners, are called Faith, Temperance, Power, and Endurance. And the others who stand
between them are Simplicity, Guilelessness, Holiness, Joy,
Truth, Understanding, Concord, and Love." "And what
are the first stones used in building the tower, which appeared from the ground?" I asked. "The first ten," he replied, "are the first generation of righteous men. The next
twenty-five are the second generation. The thirty-five
which appeared are the prophets of God. The forty are
the teachers, who spread the preaching of God's Son."
"How did they come up out of the ground without anyone quarrying them; and how were they the right shape
without anyone hewing them?" "The Church," he replied,
"was created out of nothing. It was God's Son himself
who called the first and the second generation of righteous men. It was God's Son who called the first prophets
and teachers. So no man had to guide these men in their
faith. But thereafter the members of the Church have a
duty to call others into God's kingdom to shape their
thoughts and their attitudes. The Church can only be completed by the efforts of men."

Explain to me, sir, about the mountains," I asked. "The twelve mountains," he replied, "are the tribes which inhabit the world. The twelve apostles went out to preach the Gospel of God's Son to them. But they are not tribes defined by geography or language, but rather by attitude and understanding. The first mountain, which is black, represents those who betray God by denying him when they are tested. For them, there is no repentance. The second mountain, which is bare, represents the hypocrites and heretics, who seem to teach the truth, but in fact distort the truth for their own ends. Their teaching bears no spiritual fruit. For them, there is hope if they repent quickly. The third mountain, which has thorns and thistles, represents the believers who are caught up in the affairs of the world; they are so concerned with accumulating wealth that their faith is choked. Just as it is difficult to walk with naked feet among thistles, so it is difficult for such people to enter the kingdom of God. For them, there is repentance if they retrace their steps to the moment they first believed, and then begin the journey again, but without wealth. The fourth mountain, in which the herbs growing on it are green on top but dry at their roots, represents those who are two-minded. They have the Lord on their lips, but not in their hearts; so their words are alive, but their deeds are dead. For them, there is repentance if the words on their lips slip down into their hearts."

The fifth mountain, with green herbs but rough ground, represents those who wish to know everything out of curiosity, but in fact know nothing. They pride themselves on their spiritual insights, and want to become teachers; but their desire to exalt themselves blinds them to true spiritual wisdom. Their hope lies in coming to see their own ignorance, because the admission of ignorance is the mother of knowledge. The sixth mountain which has cracks great and small with withered plants in the cracks represents those who are constantly in conflict with one another. The small cracks are those who quarrel, the large cracks are those who vent their fury at one another. The plants are their faith, which withers at such a gale of ill temper. Their hope lies in learning self-control. The seventh mountain, covered with lush grass, on which every kind of cattle and sheep and birds feed, represents those who are simple and guileless in their faith and in their actions. All who meet them are nourished by their goodness. The eighth mountain, with springs of pure water from which all sorts of creatures drink, represents the apostles and teachers, who have preached about God's Son to the world, and quench people's spiritual thirst with the pure water of truth."

The shepherd continued to explain the meaning of the mountains. "The ninth mountain, which was a desert with deadly reptiles crawling over its surface, represents the Christian leaders who exploit those in their charge. They take money even from widows, telling them that by giving money they are pleasing God; and they use the money for their own benefit. They demand that people show them respect and deference, yet do nothing to earn that respect. They may even use their position for immoral purposes. Such leaders are like deadly reptiles, devouring others; and the Churches which they lead provide no spiritual nourishment. The tenth mountain, with great trees under which sheep lie down, represent the Christian leaders who care for and protect their people, gladly welcoming them into their homes. These leaders are always eager to ensure that the destitute, the widows, and the orphans have food, shelter, and clothing. And they want no gratitude for their efforts, because they proclaim that all good things come from God. The eleventh mountain, covered with fruit trees laden with succulent fruit, represents those who have suffered for their faith in God's Son and now bear the richest spiritual fruit. All can be nourished by their wonderful example. The twelfth mountain, which is completely white, represents those who are entirely innocent, with no trace of malice or guile in their hearts. They are truly God's children, and God desires that everyone aspires to this same perfect purity."

The shepherd continued his explanation. "The stones quarried from the plain," the shepherd said, "were like stones from the white mountain. The tall man wanted to replace the bad stones with stones that will remain bright forever. Only people who have been totally innocent, like little children, are entirely indifferent to temptation; others, even apostles and those whose righteousness is famous throughout the world, are subject to temptation, and could fall. Thus the Lord chooses above all people those who can never be corrupted by wealth, power, status, or immorality, because these things have no attraction for them." "What, then," I asked, "is the meaning of the round stones, which were as bright and pure as the square stones, but could not be fit into the building?" "The round stones," the shepherd answered, "are those innocent people that are caught up in the affairs of the world, not because they desire to do so, but because they are being exploited by others, and they themselves are too guileless to understand this. Many such people are rich, having received their wealth from their parents; and rather than having the courage to give their wealth to those in need, they have allowed unscrupulous people to take charge of it. They shall soon be made poor, not because others have benefited from their generosity, but because dishonest people have taken their wealth. In becoming poor they shall have worldly vanities cast away from them, and they shall be made ready to fit into the building."

I now felt I understood the full meaning of the things which the shepherd had shown me. The shepherd then took me back to my home and sat with me. "Your task in this life," the shepherd said, "is to make yourself worthy to be a stone in that tower. You must learn to live in such a way that you fit perfectly into the Church. And once you have become part of the tower, you must not at a later time of testing be found bad and rotten, because then you will be taken out and thrown away. Those who become part of the tower must know that sin is a thing of the past. When you become part of the tower, you are giving back to God the soul which he gave to you. If you give to the dyer a new garment without fault, and he returns it to you torn, will you accept it? Surely you would become angry and demand from him compensation for the damage he has done. In the same way if you offer back to God your soul, when it is torn by sin, he will demand terrible compensation. Thus when you become part of the Church, your soul must be blameless, and remain blameless for the rest of your life on earth." The shepherd paused, and then turned to me. "You have forgotten to ask me one question," he said. "What is that?" I asked. "You have not inquired about the marks around the tower which had to be made smooth with lime and clay." "What are they?" "The sins of the people. When the stones were put in the tower, the marks they had left in the ground were wiped out. In the same way the Lord will erase all record of past sins when people enter his Church."

The angel, who had first handed me over to the shepherd, now appeared in my house. The angel stood facing me while I sat on the couch, and the shepherd stood at his right side. "I have handed you and your house to the shepherd," the angel said, "in order that you might be protected by him." "I am deeply grateful," I replied. "If, then," the angel continued, "you wish to be protected from all anxiety and cruelty, be successful in all your good works, and to grow in virtue and righteousness, follow the commandments which the shepherd has given you. If you follow his commandments, you will no longer be the slave of temptation, but its master; evil desires will have no power over you. You are now ripe for such obedience: your heart and your mind are ready for holiness. Repent now of all your past sins, and let the shepherd be your guide." The angel paused and looked at me in silence for a long time. I did not feel uneasy or awkward, but calm and peaceful; and I could feel great spiritual strength rising within me. Then the angel broke the silence. "Do you shrink from this call to holiness," the angel asked, "or do you wish to answer it?" I knew what my answer was, but I needed to wait a few moments longer before I could speak it.

The angel pressed me. "Do you shrink from the call to holiness," the angel repeated, "or do you wish to answer it?" "Before I answer your question," I replied, "I must first put a question to you. Since the shepherd has been with me, have I done anything that has offended him?" "You have done nothing to offend him," the angel replied, "because you have obeyed his commands. He has given a good account of you. Indeed he has even specially commended you to me." "Why is that?" I asked. "Because of your thirst to understand the mysteries of God," he answered. "But," I said, "he constantly showed exasperation at my questions." "He showed exasperation in order to test you. But you refused to be put off; because your thirst for divine knowledge is so strong." "If that is the case," I said, "I can answer your question. I do not shrink from the call to holiness, but wish to answer that call. I myself feel that I have constantly been offending the shepherd by my questions, yet I cannot overcome my thirst for divine knowledge. I can, with the shepherd's help, overcome every other desire, but this one is beyond my control. You tell me, however, that this is the one uncontrolled desire which is not a sin; on the contrary, it is a virtue, for which I am commended. With that assurance I am confident that I can be a willing disciple of God's Son."

The angel now put his hand on my head. "You have a great and important ministry," the angel said, "for which you will require courage in large measure. The same persistence which you have shown in discovering the truth you must now show in proclaiming the truth. Your task is to tell people the commandments of God, which the shepherd has related to you, and then to assure them that if they follow these commandments they shall be happy in this life. Many will try to destroy you, both with evil words and with violent acts. The reason for their antagonism toward you will not be because of their addiction to worldly pleasure; it will be because they know in their hearts that this addiction is wrong. So your words will stir their consciences, setting their consciences and their desires at war with each other; and they will imagine that by destroying you, their consciences will rest easy again. If they had no consciences, words of righteousness would not threaten or anger them. But you must stand firm, and speak the truth regardless of the consequences; and God will protect you." These final words of the angel frightened me, because I did not believe I had sufficient courage for this ministry. "Why," I asked, "have I been chosen for this ministry of telling others about God's commandments?" "You have not been specially chosen," the angel replied; "every follower of God's Son is chosen to proclaim the truth in word and deed."

About the Author

Robert Van de Weyer is an Anglican priest and the founder of the modern-day spiritual center which is patterned after an earlier community established in 1626 at Little Gidding, near Cambridge, England, by Nicholas Ferrar. Like the earlier foundation, the community attracts both families and singles, who follow a simple rule and practice of prayer.

Among the many works that Robert Van de Weyer has compiled are *Daily Readings with Søren Kierkegaard*; *Daily Readings with Blaise Pascal*; *The HarperCollins Book of Prayers: A Treasury of Prayers Through the Ages*; *Feasts and Fasts: A Cycle of Readings for Advent, Christmas, Lent, Easter and Pentecost*; and *On Living Simply: The Golden Voice of Saint John Chrysostom*.

Also from Triumph™ Books

Triumph Christian Thinkers

These volumes provide stimulating and accessible introductions to the lives and works of the most influential Christian thinkers who will continue to shape our spiritual heritage into the next century. Each contains essential details of biography and thought, expert appraisal of the contribution of each, and is based on up-to-date scholarship. Included are the following: